WITHDRAWN

# Other Books by Jeff Kinney

# DIARY
## of a
# Wimpy Kid

## GREG HEFFLEY'S JOURNAL

## BY JEFF KINNEY

**THORNDIKE PRESS**

A part of Gale, a Cengage Company

## GALE
A Cengage Company

Farmington Hills, Mich • Andover, UK • Chicago • Mason, Ohio
:riden, Conn • New York • San Francisco • Singapore • Waterville, Mai

**LIBRARY OF CONGRESS CATALOGING-IN-PUBLICATION DATA**

Names: Kinney, Jeff, author.
Title: Diary of a wimpy kid : Greg Heffley's journal / by Jeff Kinney.
Other titles: Greg Heffley's journal
Description: Waterville, Maine : Thorndike Press, 2017. | "Thorndike Press Large Print Mini-Collections"--Copyright page. | Originally published in a slightly different form by Amulet Books in 2007. | Summary: Greg records his sixth grade experiences in a middle school where he and his best friend, Rowley, undersized weaklings amid boys who need to shave twice daily, hope just to survive, but when Rowley grows more popular, Greg must take drastic measures to save their friendship.
Identifiers: LCCN 2016053309| ISBN 9781410498779 (hardback) | ISBN 1410498778 (hardcover)
Subjects: LCSH: Large type books. | CYAC: Middle schools--Fiction. | Friendship--Fiction. | Schools--Fiction. | Diaries--Fiction. | Humorous stories. | Large type books. | BISAC: JUVENILE FICTION / Social Issues / Friendship. | JUVENILE FICTION / Humorous Stories.
Classification: LCC PZ7.K6232 Di 2017 | DDC [Fic]--dc23
LC record available at https://lccn.loc.gov/2016053309

Published in 2017 by arrangement with Amulet Books, an imprint of Harry N. Abrams, Inc.

Printed in Mexico
5 6 7 8 9 23 22 21 20 19

TO MOM, DAD, RE, SCOTT,
AND PATRICK

<u>Tuesday</u>

First of all, let me get something straight:
This is a JOURNAL, not a diary. I know
what it says on the cover, but when Mom went
out to buy this thing I SPECIFICALLY
told her to get one that didn't say "diary"
on it.

Great. All I need is for some jerk to catch
me carrying this book around and get the
wrong idea.

The other thing I want to clear up right away
is that this was MOM's idea, not mine.

But if she thinks I'm going to write down
my "feelings" in here or whatever, she's
crazy. So just don't expect me to be all
"Dear Diary" this and "Dear Diary" that.

The only reason I agreed to do this at all is because I figure later on when I'm rich and famous, I'll have better things to do than answer people's stupid questions all day long. So this book is gonna come in handy.

Like I said, I'll be famous one day, but for now I'm stuck in middle school with a bunch of morons.

Let me just say for the record that I think middle school is the dumbest idea ever invented. You got kids like me who haven't hit their growth spurt yet mixed in with these gorillas who need to shave twice a day.

And then they wonder why bullying is such a big problem in middle school.

If it was up to me, grade levels would be based on height, not age. But then again, I guess that would mean kids like Chirag Gupta would still be in the first grade.

Today is the first day of school, and right now we're just waiting around for the teacher to hurry up and finish the seating chart. So I figured I might as well write in this book to pass the time.

By the way, let me give you some good advice. On the first day of school, you got to be real careful where you sit. You walk into the classroom and just plunk your stuff down on any old desk and the next thing you know the teacher is saying —

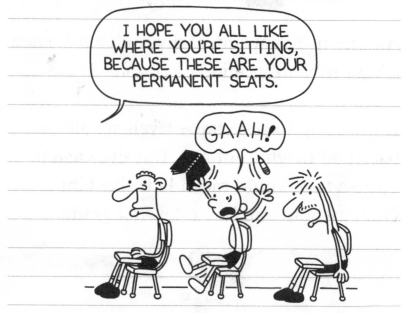

So in this class, I got stuck with Chris Hosey in front of me and Lionel James in back of me.

Jason Brill came in late and almost sat to my right, but luckily I stopped that from happening at the last second.

Next period, I should just sit in the middle of a bunch of hot girls as soon as I step in the room. But I guess if I do that, it just proves I didn't learn anything from last year.

Man, I don't know WHAT is up with girls these days. It used to be a whole lot simpler back in elementary school. The deal was, if you were the fastest runner in your class, you got all the girls.

And in the fifth grade, the fastest runner was Ronnie McCoy.

Nowadays, it's a whole lot more complicated. Now it's about the kind of clothes you wear or how rich you are or if you have a cute butt or whatever. And kids like Ronnie McCoy are scratching their heads wondering what the heck happened.

The most popular boy in my grade is Bryce Anderson. The thing that really stinks is that I have ALWAYS been into girls, but kids like Bryce have only come around in the last couple of years.

I remember how Bryce used to act back in elementary school.

But of course now I don't get any credit for sticking with the girls all this time.

Like I said, Bryce is the most popular kid in our grade, so that leaves all the rest of us guys scrambling for the other spots.

The best I can figure is that I'm somewhere around 52nd or 53rd most popular this year. But the good news is that I'm about to move up one spot because Charlie Davies is above me, and he's getting his braces next week.

I try to explain all this popularity stuff to my friend Rowley (who is probably hovering right around the 150 mark, by the way), but I think it just goes in one ear and out the other with him.

Wednesday

Today we had Phys Ed, so the first thing I did when I got outside was sneak off to the basketball court to see if the Cheese was still there. And sure enough, it was.

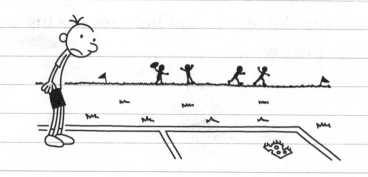

That piece of Cheese has been sitting on the blacktop since last spring. I guess it must've dropped out of someone's sandwich or something. After a couple of days, the Cheese started getting all moldy and nasty. Nobody would play basketball on the court where the Cheese was, even though that was the only court that had a hoop with a net.

Then one day, this kid named Darren Walsh touched the Cheese with his finger, and that's what started this thing called the Cheese Touch. It's basically like the Cooties. If you get the Cheese Touch, you're stuck with it until you pass it on to someone else.

The only way to protect yourself from the Cheese Touch is to cross your fingers.

But it's not that easy remembering to keep your fingers crossed every moment of the day. I ended up taping mine together so they'd stay crossed all the time. I got a D in handwriting, but it was totally worth it.

This one kid named Abe Hall got the Cheese Touch in April, and nobody would even come near him for the rest of the year. This summer Abe moved away to California and took the Cheese Touch with him.

I just hope someone doesn't start the Cheese Touch up again, because I don't need that kind of stress in my life anymore.

<u>Thursday</u>
I'm having a seriously hard time getting used to the fact that summer is over and I have to get out of bed every morning to go to school.

My summer did not exactly get off to a great start, thanks to my older brother Rodrick.

16

A couple of days into summer vacation, Rodrick woke me up in the middle of the night. He told me I slept through the whole summer, but that luckily I woke up just in time for the first day of school.

You might think I was pretty dumb for falling for that one, but Rodrick was dressed up in his school clothes and he set my alarm clock ahead to make it look like it was the morning. Plus, he closed my curtains so I couldn't see that it was still dark out.

After Rodrick woke me up, I just got dressed and went downstairs to make myself some breakfast, like I do every morning on a school day.

But I guess I must have made a pretty big racket because the next thing I knew, Dad was downstairs, yelling at me for eating Cheerios at 3:00 in the morning.

It took me a minute to figure out what the heck was going on.

After I did, I told Dad that Rodrick had played a trick on me, and HE was the one that should be getting yelled at.

Dad walked down to the basement to chew Rodrick out, and I tagged along. I couldn't wait to see Rodrick get what was coming to him.

But Rodrick covered up his tracks pretty good. And to this day, I'm sure Dad thinks I've got a screw loose or something.

Friday
Today at school we got assigned to reading groups.

They don't come right out and tell you if you're in the Gifted group or the Easy group, but you can figure it out right away by looking at the covers of the books they hand out.

I was pretty disappointed to find out I got put in the Gifted group, because that just means a lot of extra work.

When they did the screening at the end of last year, I did my best to make sure I got put in the Easy group this year.

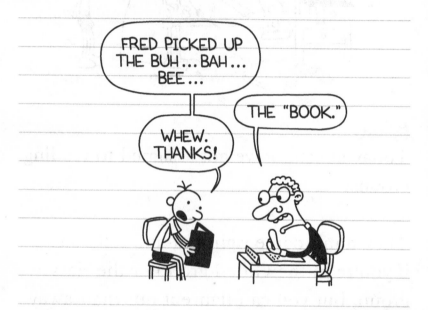

Mom is real tight with our principal, so I'll bet she stepped in and made sure I got put in the Gifted group again.

Mom is always saying I'm a smart kid, but that I just don't "apply" myself.

But if there's one thing I learned from Rodrick, it's to set people's expectations real low so you end up surprising them by practically doing nothing at all.

Actually, I'm kind of glad my plan to get put in the Easy group didn't work.

I saw a couple of the "Bink Says Boo" kids holding their books upside down, and I don't think they were joking.

Saturday
Well, the first week of school is finally over, so today I slept in.

Most kids wake up early on Saturday to watch cartoons or whatever, but not me. The only reason I get out of bed at all on weekends is because eventually, I can't stand the taste of my own breath anymore.

Unfortunately, Dad wakes up at 6:00 in the morning no matter WHAT day of the week it is, and he is not real considerate of the fact that I am trying to enjoy my Saturday like a normal person.

I didn't have anything to do today so I just headed up to Rowley's house.

Rowley is technically my best friend, but that is definitely subject to change.

I've been avoiding Rowley since the first day of school, when he did something that really annoyed me.

We were getting our stuff from our lockers at the end of the day, and Rowley came up to me and said —

I have told Rowley at least a billion times that now that we're in middle school, you're supposed to say "hang out," not "play." But no matter how many noogies I give him, he always forgets the next time.

I've been trying to be a lot more careful about my image ever since I got to middle school. But having Rowley around is definitely not helping.

I met Rowley a few years ago when he moved into my neighborhood.

His mom bought him this book called "How to Make Friends in New Places," and he came to my house trying all these dumb gimmicks.

I guess I kind of felt sorry for Rowley, and I decided to take him under my wing.

It's been great having him around, mostly because I get to use all the tricks Rodrick pulls on ME.

<u>Monday</u>

You know how I said I play all sorts of pranks on Rowley? Well, I have a little brother named Manny, and I could NEVER get away with pulling any of that stuff on him.

Mom and Dad protect Manny like he's a prince or something. And he never gets in trouble, even if he really deserves it.

Yesterday, Manny drew a self-portrait on my bedroom door in permanent marker. I thought Mom and Dad were really going to let him have it, but as usual, I was wrong.

But the thing that bugs me the most about Manny is the nickname he has for me. When he was a baby, he couldn't pronounce "brother," so he started calling me "Bubby." And he STILL calls me that now, even though I keep trying to get Mom and Dad to make him stop.

Luckily none of my friends have found out yet, but believe me, I have had some really close calls.

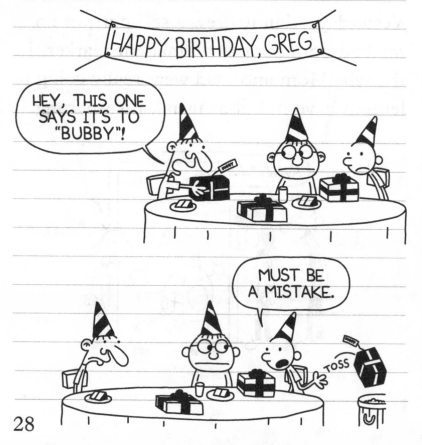

Mom makes me help Manny get ready for
school in the morning. After I make Manny
his breakfast, he carries his cereal bowl
into the family room and sits on his plastic
potty.

And when it's time for him to go to day
care, he gets up and dumps whatever he
didn't eat right in the toilet.

Mom is always getting on me about not
finishing my breakfast. But if she had to
scrape corn flakes out of the bottom of a
plastic potty every morning, she wouldn't
have much of an appetite either.

<u>Tuesday</u>

I don't know if I mentioned this before, but I am SUPER good at video games. I'll bet I could beat anyone in my grade head-to-head.

Unfortunately, Dad does not exactly appreciate my skills. He's always getting on me about going out and doing something "active."

So tonight after dinner when Dad started hassling me about going outside, I tried to explain how with video games, you can play sports like football and soccer, and you don't even get all hot and sweaty.

But as usual, Dad didn't see my logic.

Dad is a pretty smart guy in general but when it comes to common sense, sometimes I wonder about him.

I'm sure Dad would dismantle my game system if he could figure out how to do it. But luckily, the people who make these things make them parent-proof.

Every time Dad kicks me out of the house to do something sporty, I just go up to Rowley's and play my video games there.

Unfortunately, the only games I can play at Rowley's are car-racing games and stuff like that.

Because whenever I bring a game up to Rowley's house, his dad looks it up on some parents' Web site. And if my game has ANY kind of fighting or violence in it, he won't let us play.

I'm getting a little sick of playing Formula One Racing with Rowley, because he's not a serious gamer like me. All that you have to do to beat Rowley is name your car something ridiculous at the beginning of the game.

And then when you pass Rowley's car, he just falls to pieces.

Anyway, after I got done mopping the floor with Rowley today, I headed home. I ran through the neighbor's sprinkler a couple times to make it look like I was all sweaty, and that seemed to do the trick for Dad.

But my trick kind of backfired, because as soon as Mom saw me, she made me go upstairs and take a shower.

Wednesday

I guess Dad must have been pretty happy with himself for making me go outside yesterday, because he did it again today.

It's getting really annoying to have to go up to Rowley's every time I want to play a video game. There's this weird kid named Fregley who lives halfway between my house and Rowley's, and Fregley is always hanging out in his front yard. So it's pretty hard to avoid him.

Fregley is in my Phys Ed class at school, and he has this whole made-up language. Like when he needs to go to the bathroom, he says —

Us kids have pretty much figured Fregley out by now, but I don't think the teachers have really caught on yet.

Today, I probably would have gone up to Rowley's on my own anyway, because my brother Rodrick and his band were practicing down in the basement.

Rodrick's band is REALLY awful, and I can't stand being home when they're having rehearsals.

His band is called "Loaded Diaper," only it's spelled "Löded Diper" on Rodrick's van.

You might think he spelled it that way to make it look cooler, but I bet if you told Rodrick how "Loaded Diaper" is really spelled, it would be news to him.

Dad was against the idea of Rodrick starting a band, but Mom was all for it.

She's the one who bought Rodrick his first drum set.

I think Mom has this idea that we're all going to learn to play instruments and then become one of those family bands like you see on TV.

Dad really hates heavy metal, and that's the kind of music Rodrick and his band play. I don't think Mom really cares what Rodrick plays or listens to, because to her, all music is the same. In fact, earlier today, Rodrick was listening to one of his CDs in the family room, and Mom came in and started dancing.

That really bugged Rodrick, so he drove off
to the store and came back fifteen minutes
later with some headphones. And that
pretty much took care of the problem.

Thursday
Yesterday Rodrick got a new heavy metal
CD, and it had one of those "Parental
Warning" stickers on it.

I have never gotten to listen to one of those
Parental Warning CDs, because Mom and
Dad never let me buy them at the mall. So
I realized the only way I was gonna get a
chance to listen to Rodrick's CD was if I
snuck it out of the house.

This morning, after Rodrick left, I called
up Rowley and told him to bring his CD
player to school.
38

Then I went down to Rodrick's room and took the CD off his rack.

You're not allowed to bring personal music players to school, so we had to wait to use it until after lunch when the teachers let us outside. As soon as we got the chance, me and Rowley snuck around the back of the school and loaded up Rodrick's CD.

But Rowley forgot to put batteries in his CD player, so it was pretty much worthless.

Then I came up with this great idea for a game. The object was to put the headphones on your head and then try to shake them off without using your hands.

The winner was whoever could shake the headphones off in the shortest amount of time.

I had the record with seven and a half seconds, but I think I might have shook some of my fillings loose with that one.

Right in the middle of our game, Mrs. Craig came around the corner and caught us red-handed. She took the music player away from me and started chewing us out.

But I think she had the wrong idea about what we were doing back there. She started telling us how rock and roll is "evil" and how it's going to ruin our brains.

I was going to tell her that there weren't even any batteries in the CD player, but I could tell she didn't want to be interrupted. So I just waited until she was done, and then I said, "Yes, ma'am."

But right when Mrs. Craig was about to let us go, Rowley started blubbering about how he doesn't want rock and roll to ruin his "brains."

Honestly, sometimes I don't know about that boy.

<u>Friday</u>

Well, now I've gone and done it.

Last night, after everyone was in bed, I
snuck downstairs to listen to Rodrick's CD
on the stereo in the family room.

I put Rodrick's new headphones on and
cranked up the volume REALLY high.
Then I hit "play."

First, let me just say I can definitely
understand why they put that "Parental
Warning" sticker on the CD.

But I only got to hear about thirty seconds
of the first song before I got interrupted.

It turns out I didn't have the headphones plugged into the stereo. So the music was actually coming through the SPEAKERS, not the headphones.

Dad marched me up to my room and shut the door behind him, and then he said —

Whenever Dad says "friend" that way, you know you're in trouble. The first time Dad ever said "friend" like that to me, I didn't get that he was being sarcastic. So I kind of let my guard down.

I don't make that mistake anymore.

Tonight, Dad yelled at me for about ten minutes, and then I guess he decided he'd rather be in bed than standing in my room in his underwear. He told me I was grounded from playing video games for two weeks, which is about what I expected. I guess I should be glad that's all he did.

The good thing about Dad is that when he gets mad, he cools off real quick, and then it's over.

Usually, if you mess up in front of Dad, he just throws whatever he's got in his hands at you.

GOOD TIME TO SCREW UP:

KICK

BAD TIME TO SCREW UP:

KICK

Mom has a TOTALLY different style when it comes to punishment. If you mess up and Mom catches you, the first thing she does is to take a few days to figure out what your punishment should be.

And while you're waiting, you do all these nice things to try to get off easier.

But then after a few days, right when YOU forget you're in trouble, that's when she lays it on you.

<u>Monday</u>

This video game ban is a whole lot tougher than I thought it would be. But at least I'm not the only one in the family who's in trouble.

Rodrick's in some hot water with Mom right now, too. Manny got ahold of one of Rodrick's heavy metal magazines, and one of the pages had a picture of a woman in a bikini lying across the hood of a car. And then Manny brought it into day care for show-and-tell.

Anyway, I don't think Mom was too happy about getting that phone call.

I saw the magazine myself, and it honestly wasn't anything to get worked up over. But Mom doesn't allow that kind of stuff in the house.

Rodrick's punishment was that he had to answer a bunch of questions Mom wrote out for him.

Did owning this magazine make you a better person?

No.

Did it make you more popular at school?

No.

How do you feel about having owned this type of magazine now?

I feel ashamed.

Do you have anything you want to say to women for having owned this offensive magazine?

I'm sorry women.

Wednesday

I'm still grounded from playing video games, so Manny has been using my system. Mom went out and bought a whole bunch of educational video games, and watching Manny play them is like torture.

The good news is that I finally figured out how to get some of my games past Rowley's dad. I just put one of my discs in Manny's "Discovering the Alphabet" case, and that's all it takes.

## Thursday

At school today, they announced that student government elections are coming up. To be honest with you, I've never had any interest in student government. But when I started thinking about it, I realized getting elected Treasurer could TOTALLY change my situation at school.

And even better . . .

Nobody ever thinks about running for Treasurer, because all anyone ever cares about are the big-ticket positions like President and Vice President. So I figure if I sign up tomorrow, the Treasurer job is pretty much mine for the taking.

Friday
Today, I went and put my name on the list to run for Treasurer. Unfortunately, this kid named Marty Porter is running for Treasurer, too, and he's real brainy at math. So this might not be as easy as I thought.

I told Dad that I was running for student government, and he seemed pretty excited. It turns out he ran for student government when he was my age, and he actually won.

Dad dug through some old boxes in the basement and found one of his campaign posters.

INTEGRITY
HONESTY
KNOW-HOW

V★TE
Frank Heffley
FOR
SECRETARY

I thought the poster idea was pretty good, so I asked Dad to drive me to the store to get some supplies. I loaded up on poster board and markers, and I spent the rest of the night making all my campaign stuff. So let's just hope these posters work.

<u>Monday</u>
I brought my posters in to school today, and I have to say, they came out pretty good.

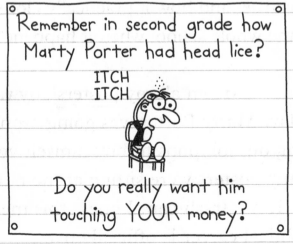

I started hanging my posters up as soon as I got in. But they were only up for about three minutes before Vice Principal Roy spotted them.

Mr. Roy said you weren't allowed to write "fabrications" about the other candidates. So I told Mr. Roy that the thing about the head lice was true, and how it practically closed down the whole school when it happened.

But he took down all my posters anyway. So today, Marty Porter was going around handing out lollipops to buy himself votes while my posters were sitting at the bottom of Mr. Roy's trash can. I guess this means my political career is officially over.

<u>Monday</u>

Well, it's finally October, and there are only thirty days left until Halloween. Halloween is my FAVORITE holiday, even though Mom says I'm getting too old to go trick-or-treating anymore.

Halloween is Dad's favorite holiday, too, but for a different reason. On Halloween night, while all the other parents are handing out candy, Dad is hiding in the bushes with a big trash can full of water.

And if any teenagers pass by our driveway, he drenches them.

I'm not sure Dad really understands the concept of Halloween. But I'm not gonna be the one who spoils his fun.

Tonight was the opening night of the Crossland High School haunted house, and I got Mom to agree to take me and Rowley.

Rowley showed up at my house wearing his Halloween costume from last year. When I called him earlier I told him to just wear regular clothes, but of course he didn't listen.

I tried not to let it bother me too much, though. I've never been allowed to go to the Crossland haunted house before, and I wasn't going to let Rowley ruin it for me. Rodrick has told me all about it, and I've been looking forward to this for about three years.

Anyway, when we got to the entrance, I started having second thoughts about going in.

GOOD EEEVENINGGG.

But Mom seemed like she was in a hurry to get this over with, and she moved us along. Once we were through the gate, it was one scare after another. There were vampires jumping out at you and people without heads and all sorts of crazy stuff.

But the worst part was this area called
Chainsaw Alley. There was this big guy in a
hockey mask and he had a REAL chainsaw.
Rodrick told me the chainsaw has a rubber
blade, but I wasn't taking any chances.

Right when it looked like the chainsaw guy
was going to catch us, Mom stepped in and
bailed us out.

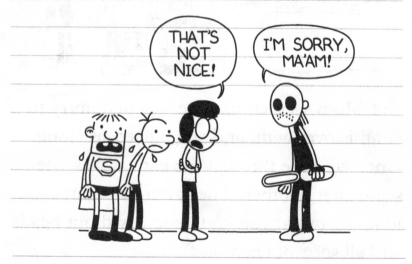

Mom made the chainsaw guy show us where the exit was, and that was the end of our haunted house experience right there. I guess it was a little embarrassing when Mom did that, but I'm willing to let it go this one time.

Saturday
The Crossland haunted house really got me thinking. Those guys were charging five bucks a pop, and the line stretched halfway around the school.

I decided to make a haunted house of my own. Actually, I had to bring Rowley in on the deal, because Mom wouldn't let me convert our first floor into a full-out haunted mansion.

I knew Rowley's dad wouldn't be crazy about the idea, either, so we decided to build the haunted house in his basement and just not mention it to his parents.

Me and Rowley spent most of the day coming up with an awesome plan for our haunted house.

Here was our final plan:

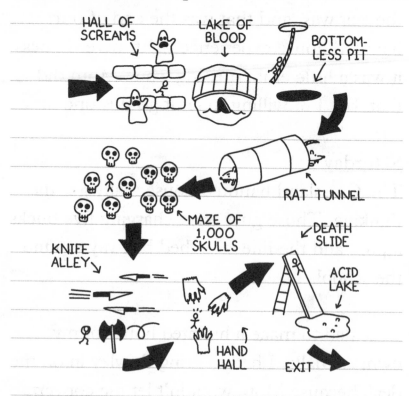

I don't mean to brag or anything, but what we came up with was WAY better than the Crossland High School haunted house.

We realized we were gonna need to get the word out that we were doing this thing, so we got some paper and made up a bunch of flyers.

I'll admit maybe we stretched the truth a little in our advertisement, but we had to make sure people actually showed up.

HAUNTED
H☠USE
OUCH.
WITH **LIVE** SHARKS!

32 SURREY STREET
ADMISSION: 50¢
3:00 p.m.

By the time we finished putting the flyers up around the neighborhood and got back to Rowley's basement, it was already 2:30, and we hadn't even started putting the actual haunted house together yet.

So we had to cut some corners from our original plan.

When 3:00 rolled around, we looked outside to see if anyone had showed up. And sure enough, there were about twenty neighborhood kids waiting in line outside Rowley's basement.

Now, I know our flyers said admission was fifty cents, but I could see that we had a chance to make a killing here.

So I told the kids that admission was two bucks, and the fifty-cent thing was just a typo.

The first kid to cough up his two bucks was Shane Snella. He paid his money and we let him inside, and me and Rowley took our positions in the Hall of Screams.

The Hall of Screams was basically a bed with me and Rowley on either side of it.

I guess maybe we made the Hall of Screams a little too scary, because halfway through, Shane curled up in a ball underneath the bed. We tried to get him to crawl out from under there, but he wouldn't budge.

I started thinking about all the money we were losing with this kid clogging up the Hall of Screams, and I knew we had to get him out of there, quick.

Eventually, Rowley's dad came downstairs. At first I was happy to see him, because I thought he could help us drag Shane out from under the bed and get our haunted house cranking again.

But Rowley's dad wasn't really in a helpful mood.

Rowley's dad wanted to know what we were doing, and why Shane Snella was curled up under the bed.

We told him that the basement was a haunted house, and that Shane Snella actually PAID for us to do this to him. But Rowley's dad didn't believe us.

I admit that if you looked around, it didn't really look like a haunted house. All we had time to put together was the Hall of Screams and the Lake of Blood, which was just Rowley's old baby pool with half a bottle of ketchup in it.

64

I tried to show Rowley's dad our original plan to prove that we really were running a legitimate operation, but he still didn't seem convinced.

And to make a long story short, that was the end of our haunted house.

The good news is, since Rowley's dad didn't believe us, he didn't make us refund Shane's money. So at least we cleared two bucks today.

<u>Sunday</u>

Rowley ended up getting grounded for that whole haunted house mess yesterday. He's not allowed to watch TV for a week, AND he's not allowed to have me over at his house during that time.

That last part really isn't fair, because that's punishing me, and I didn't even do anything wrong. And now where am I supposed to play my video games?

Anyway, I felt kind of bad for Rowley. So tonight, I tried to make it up to him. I turned on one of Rowley's favorite TV shows, and I did a play-by-play over the phone so he could kind of experience it that way.

WOW! LOOK AT THE SIZE OF THAT FLAMETHROWER!

OH YEAH, NEVER MIND.

I did my best to keep up with what was
going on on the screen, but to be honest
with you, I'm not sure if Rowley was
getting the full effect.

Tuesday

Well, Rowley's grounding is finally over,
and just in time for Halloween, too. I went
up to his house to check out his costume,
and I have to admit, I'm a little jealous.

Rowley's Mom got him this knight costume
that's WAY cooler than his costume from
last year.

His knight outfit came with a helmet and a
shield and a real sword and EVERYTHING.

I've never had a store-bought costume
before. I still haven't figured out what
I'm gonna go as tomorrow night, so I'll
probably just throw something together at
the last minute. I figure maybe I'll bring
back the Toilet Paper Mummy again.

But I think it's supposed to rain tomorrow
night, so that might not be the smartest
choice.

In the past few years, the grown-ups in my neighborhood have been getting cranky about my lame costumes, and I'm starting to think it's actually having an effect on the amount of candy I'm bringing in.

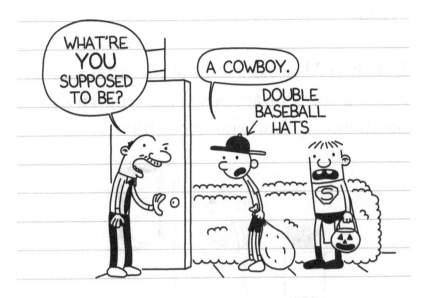

But I don't really have time to put together a good costume, because I'm in charge of planning out the best route for me and Rowley to take tomorrow night.

This year I've come up with a plan that'll get us at least twice the candy we scored last year.

## Halloween

About an hour before we were supposed
to start trick-or-treating, I still didn't have
a costume. At that point I was seriously
thinking about going as a cowboy for the
second year in a row.

But then Mom knocked at my door and
handed me a pirate costume, with an eye
patch and a hook and everything.

Rowley showed up around 6:30 wearing
his knight costume, but it didn't look
ANYTHING like it looked yesterday.

Rowley's mom made all these safety
improvements to it, and you couldn't even
tell what he was supposed to be anymore.

She cut out a big hole in the front of the
helmet so he could see better, and covered
him up in all this reflective tape. She made
him wear his winter coat underneath
everything, and she replaced his sword with
a glow stick.

I grabbed my pillowcase, and me and
Rowley started to head out. But Mom
stopped us before we could get out the door.

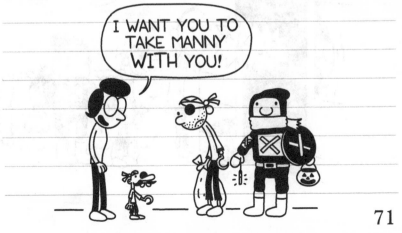

Man, I should have known there was a catch when Mom gave me that costume.

I told Mom there was no WAY we were taking Manny with us, because we were going to hit 152 houses in three hours. And plus, we were going to be on Snake Road, which is way too dangerous for a little kid like Manny.

I should never have mentioned that last part, because the next thing I knew, Mom was telling Dad he had to go along with us to make sure we didn't step foot outside our neighborhood. Dad tried to squirm out of it, but once Mom makes up her mind, there's no way you can change it.

Before we even got out of our own driveway, we ran into our neighbor Mr. Mitchell and his kid Jeremy. So of course THEY tagged along with us.

Manny and Jeremy wouldn't trick-or-treat at any houses with spooky decorations on them, so that ruled out pretty much every house on our block.

Dad and Mr. Mitchell started talking about football or something, and every time one of them wanted to make a point, they'd stop walking.

BLAH BLAH
BLAH BLAH
BLAH BLAH

BLAH BLAH
BLAH BLAH
BLAH BLAH

So we were hitting only about one house every twenty minutes.

After a couple of hours, Dad and Mr. Mitchell took the little kids home.

I was glad, because that meant me and Rowley could take off. My pillowcase was almost empty, so I wanted to make up as much time as possible.

A little while later, Rowley told me he needed a "potty break." I made him hold off for another forty-five minutes. But by the time we got to my gramma's house, it was pretty clear that if I didn't let Rowley use the bathroom, it was gonna get messy.

So I told Rowley if he wasn't back outside in one minute, I was gonna start helping myself to his candy.

After that, we headed back out on the road. But it was already 10:30, and I guess that's when most grown-ups decide Halloween is over.

You can kind of tell because that's when they start coming to the door in their pajamas and giving you the evil eye.

We decided to head home. We made up a lot of time after Dad and Manny left, so I was pretty satisfied with how much candy we took in.

When we were halfway home, this pickup truck came roaring down the street with a bunch of high school kids in it.

The kid in the back was holding a fire extinguisher, and when the truck passed by us, he opened fire.

I have to give Rowley credit, because he blocked about 95% of the water with his shield. And if he hadn't done that, all our candy would have gotten soaked.

When the truck drove away, I yelled out something that I regretted about two seconds later.

The driver slammed on the brakes and he turned his truck around. Me and Rowley started running, but those guys were right on our heels.

The only place I could think of that was safe was Gramma's house, so we cut through a couple backyards to get there. Gramma was in bed already, but I knew she keeps a key under the mat on her front porch.

Once we got inside, I looked out the window to see if those guys had followed us, and sure enough, they did. I tried to trick them into leaving, but they wouldn't budge.

WELL, I GUESS NOW THAT WE'RE SAFE IN OUR OWN HOUSE, YOU CAN'T GET US!

After a while, we realized the teenagers were going to wait us out, so we decided we were just gonna have to spend the night at Gramma's. That's when we started getting cocky, making monkey noises at the teenagers and whatnot.

Well, at least I was making monkey noises. Rowley was kind of making owl noises, but I guess it was the same general idea.

I called Mom to tell her we were going to crash at Gramma's for the night. But Mom sounded really mad on the phone.

She said it was a school night, and that we had to get home right that instant. So that meant we were gonna have to make a run for it.

I looked out the window, and this time, I didn't see the truck. But I knew those guys were hiding somewhere and were just trying to draw us out.

So we snuck out the back door, hopped over Gramma's fence, and ran all the way to Snake Road. I figured our chances were better there because there aren't any streetlights.

Snake Road is scary enough on its own without having a truckload of teenagers hunting you down. Every time we saw a car coming, we dove into the bushes. It must've taken us a half hour to go 100 yards.

But believe it or not, we made it all the way home without getting caught. Neither one of us let our guard down until we got to my driveway.

But right then, there was this awful scream, and we saw a big wave of water coming toward us.

Man, I forgot ALL about Dad, and we totally paid the price for it.

When me and Rowley got inside, we laid out all our candy on the kitchen table.

The only things we could salvage were a couple of mints that were wrapped in cellophane, and the toothbrushes Dr. Garrison gave us.

I think next Halloween I'll just stay home and mooch some Butterfingers from the bowl Mom keeps on top of the refrigerator.

## Thursday

On the bus ride into school today, we passed by Gramma's house. It got rolled with toilet paper last night, which I guess was no big surprise.

I do feel a little bad, because it looked like it was gonna take a long time to clean up. But on the bright side, Gramma is retired, so she probably didn't have anything planned for today anyway.

## Wednesday

In third period, Mr. Underwood, our Phys Ed teacher, announced that the boys will be doing a wrestling unit for the next six weeks.

If there's one thing most boys in my school are into, it's professional wrestling. So Mr. Underwood might as well have set off a bomb.

Lunch comes right after Phys Ed, and the cafeteria was a complete madhouse.

I don't know what the school is thinking having a wrestling unit.

But I decided if I don't want to get twisted into a pretzel for the next month and a half, I'd better do my homework on this wrestling business.

So I rented a couple of video games to
learn some moves. And you know what?
After a while, I was really starting to get the
hang of it.

In fact, the other kids in my class had
better look out, because if I keep this up, I
could be a real threat.

Then again, I better make sure I don't do TOO good. This kid named Preston Mudd got named Athlete of the Month for being the best player in the basketball unit, so they put his picture up in the hallway.

P. Mudd

Athlete of the Month

It took people about five seconds to realize how "P. Mudd" sounded when you said it out loud, and after that, it was all over for Preston.

<u>Thursday</u>
Well, I found out today that the kind of
wrestling Mr. Underwood is teaching is
COMPLETELY different from the kind
they do on TV.

First of all, we have to wear these things
called "singlets," which look like those
bathing suits they used to wear in the
1800s.

And second of all, there are no pile drivers
or hitting people over the heads with chairs
or anything like that.

There's not even a ring with ropes around
it. It's just basically a sweaty mat that
smells like it's never been washed before.

Mr. Underwood started asking for volunteers so he could demonstrate some wrestling holds, but there was no way I was going to raise my hand.

Me and Rowley tried to hide out in the back of the gym near the curtain, but that's where the girls were doing their gymnastics unit.

We got out of there in a hurry, and we went back to where the rest of the guys were.

Mr. Underwood singled me out, probably because I'm the lightest kid in the class, and he could toss me around without straining himself. He showed everybody how to do all these things called a "half nelson" and a "reversal" and a "takedown" and stuff like that.

When he was doing this one move called the "fireman's carry," I felt a breeze down below, and I could tell my singlet wasn't doing a good job keeping me covered up.

That's when I thanked my lucky stars the girls were on the other side of the gym.

Mr. Underwood divided us up into weight groups. I was pretty happy about that at first, because it meant I wasn't going to have to wrestle kids like Benny Wells, who can bench-press 250 pounds.

But then I found out who I DID have to wrestle, and I would have traded for Benny Wells in a heartbeat.

> GREG, YOU'LL BE PAIRED UP WITH FREGLEY HERE.

Fregley was the only kid light enough to be in my weight class. And apparently Fregley was paying attention when Mr. Underwood was giving instructions, because he pinned me every which way you could imagine. I spent my seventh period getting WAY more familiar with Fregley than I ever wanted to be.

> TWEET!

<u>Tuesday</u>

This wrestling unit has totally turned
our school upside down. Now kids are
wrestling in the hallways, in the classrooms,
you name it. But the fifteen minutes after
lunch where they let us outside is the
worst.

You can't walk five feet without tripping
over a couple of kids going at it. I just try
to keep my distance. And mark my words,
one of these fools is going to roll right onto
the Cheese and start the Cheese Touch all
over again.

90

My other big problem is that I have to
wrestle Fregley every single day. But this
morning I realized something. If I can
move out of Fregley's weight class, I won't
have to wrestle him anymore.

So today, I stuffed my clothes with a bunch
of socks and shirts to get myself into the
next weight class.

But I was still too light to move up.

I realized I was gonna have to gain weight
for real. At first I thought I should just start
loading up on junk food, but then I had a
much better idea.

I decided to gain my weight in MUSCLE, not fat.

I've never been all that interested in getting in shape before, but this wrestling unit has made me rethink things.

I figure if I bulk up now, it could actually come in handy down the road.

The football unit is coming in the spring, and they split the teams up into shirts and skins. And I ALWAYS get put on skins.

I think they do that to make all the out-of-shape kids feel ashamed of themselves.

UNH!

If I can pack on some muscle now, it'll be a whole different story next April.

Tonight, after dinner, I got Mom and Dad together and told them my plan. I told them I was going to need some serious exercise equipment, and some weight-gain powder, too.

I showed them some muscle magazines I got at the store so they could see how ripped I was going to be.

Mom didn't really say anything at first, but Dad was pretty enthusiastic. I think he was just glad I had a change of heart from how I used to be when I was a kid —

But Mom said if I wanted a weight set, I was going to have to prove that I could stick with an exercise regimen. She said I could do that by doing sit-ups and jumping jacks for two weeks.

I had to explain that the only way to get totally bulked up is to get the kind of high-tech machines they have at the gym, but Mom didn't want to hear it.

Then Dad said if I wanted a bench press,
I should keep my fingers crossed for
Christmas.

But Christmas is a month and a half away.
And if I get pinned by Fregley one more
time, I'm gonna have a nervous breakdown.

So it looks like Mom and Dad aren't going
to be any help. And that means I'm going
to have to take matters into my own hands,
as usual.

Saturday
I couldn't wait to start my weight-training
program today. Even though Mom wouldn't
let me get the equipment I needed, I wasn't
going to let that hold me back.

So I went into the fridge and emptied out the milk and orange juice and filled the jugs with sand. Then I taped them to a broomstick, and I had myself a pretty decent barbell.

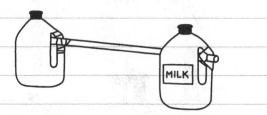

After that, I made a bench press out of an ironing board and some boxes. Once I had that all set, I was ready to do some serious lifting.

I needed a spotting partner, so I called Rowley. And when he showed up at my door wearing some ridiculous getup, I knew I made a mistake inviting him.

I made Rowley use the bench press first, mostly because I wanted to see if the broomstick was going to hold up.

He did about five reps, and he was ready to quit, but I wouldn't let him. That's what a good training partner is for, to push you beyond your limits.

I knew Rowley wasn't going to be as serious about weight lifting as I was, so I decided to try out an experiment to test his dedication.

In the middle of Rowley's set, I went and got this phony nose and mustache Rodrick has in his junk drawer.

And right when Rowley had the barbell in the "down" position, I leaned over and looked at him.

Sure enough, Rowley TOTALLY lost his concentration. He couldn't even get the barbell off his chest. I thought about helping him out, but then I realized that if Rowley didn't get serious about working out, he was never going to get to my level.

I eventually had to rescue him, because he started biting the milk jug to let the sand leak out.

After Rowley got off the bench press, it was time for my set. But Rowley said he didn't feel like working out anymore, and he went home.

You know, I figured he'd pull something like that. But I guess you can't expect everyone to have the same kind of dedication as you.

Wednesday
Today in Geography we had a quiz, and I have to say, I've been looking forward to this one for a long time.

The quiz was on state capitals, and I sit in the back of the room, right next to this giant map of the United States. All the capitals are written in big red print, so I knew I had this one in the bag.

But right before the test got started, Patty
Farrell piped up from the front of the
room.

Patty told Mr. Ira that he should cover
up the United States map before we got
started.

So thanks to Patty, I ended up flunking the
quiz. And I will definitely be looking for a
way to pay her back for that one.

<u>Thursday</u>

Tonight Mom came up to my room, and she had a flyer in her hand. As soon as I saw it, I knew EXACTLY what it was.

It was an announcement that the school is having tryouts for a winter play. Man, I should have thrown that thing out when I saw it on the kitchen table.

I BEGGED her not to make me sign up. Those school plays are always musicals, and the last thing I need is to have to sing a solo in front of the whole school.

But all my begging seemed to do was make Mom more sure I should do it.

Mom said the only way I was going to be "well-rounded" was by trying different things.

Dad came in my room to see what was going on. I told Dad that Mom was making me sign up for the school play, and that if I had to start going to play practices, it would totally mess up my weight-lifting schedule.

I knew that would make Dad take my side. Dad and Mom argued for a few minutes, but Dad was no match for Mom.

So that means tomorrow I've got to audition for the school play.

<u>Friday</u>
The play they're doing this year is "The Wizard of Oz." A lot of kids came wearing costumes for the parts they were trying out for.

I've never even seen the movie, so for me, it was like walking into a freak show.

Mrs. Norton, the music director, made everyone sing "My Country 'Tis of Thee" so she could hear our singing voices. I did my singing tryouts with a bunch of other boys whose moms made them come, too. I tried to sing as quietly as possible, but of course I got singled out, anyway.

I have no idea what a "soprano" is, but from the way some of the girls were giggling, I knew it wasn't a good thing.

Tryouts went on forever. The grand finale came with auditions for Dorothy, who I guess is the lead character in the play.

And who should try out first but Patty Farrell.

I thought about trying out for the part of the Witch, because I heard that in the play, the Witch does all sorts of mean things to Dorothy.

But then somebody told me there's a Good Witch and a Bad Witch, and with my luck, I'd end up getting picked to be the good one.

104

## Monday

I was hoping Mrs. Norton would just cut me from the play, but today she said that everyone who tried out is going to get a part. So lucky me.

Mrs. Norton showed "The Wizard of Oz" movie so everyone would know the story. I was trying to figure out what part I should play, but pretty much every character has to sing or dance at one point or another. But about halfway through the movie, I figured out what part I wanted to sign up for. I'm going to sign up to be a Tree, because 1) they don't have to sing and 2) they get to bean Dorothy with apples.

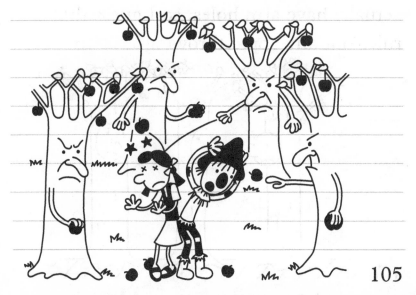

Getting to peg Patty Farrell with apples in front of a live audience would be my dream come true. I may actually have to thank Mom for making me do this play once it's all over.

After the movie ended, I signed up to be a Tree. Unfortunately, a bunch of other guys had the same idea as me, so I guess there are a lot of guys who have a bone to pick with Patty Farrell.

Wednesday
Well, like Mom always says, be careful what you wish for. I got picked to be a Tree, but I don't know if that's such a good thing. The Tree costumes don't actually have arm holes, so I guess that rules out any apple-throwing.

I should probably feel lucky that I got a speaking part at all. They had too many kids trying out, and not enough roles, so they had to start making up characters.

Rodney James tried out to be the Tin Man, but he got stuck with being the Shrub.

Friday

Remember how I said I was lucky to get a speaking part? Well, today I found out I only have one line in the whole play. I say it when Dorothy picks an apple off my branch.

OUCH.

PLUCK

That means I have to go to a two-hour practice every day just so I can say one stupid word.

I'm starting to think Rodney James got a better deal as the Shrub. He found a way to sneak a video game into his costume, and I'll bet that really makes the time go by.

So now I'm trying to think of ways to get Mrs. Norton to kick me out of the play. But when you only have one word to say, it's really hard to mess up your lines.

Thursday

The play is only a couple of days away, and I have no idea how we're going to pull this thing off.

First of all, nobody has bothered to learn their lines, and that's all Mrs. Norton's fault.

During rehearsal, Mrs. Norton whispers everyone's lines to them from the side of the stage.

I wonder how it's going to go next Tuesday when Mrs. Norton is sitting at her piano thirty feet away.

Another thing that's screwing everything up is that Mrs. Norton keeps adding new scenes and new characters.

Yesterday, she brought in this first-grader to play Dorothy's dog, Toto. But today, the kid's mom came in and said she wanted her child to walk around on two legs, because crawling around on all fours would be too "degrading."

So now we've got a dog that's gonna be walking around on his hind legs for the whole show.

But the worst change is that Mrs. Norton actually wrote a song that us TREES have to sing. She said everyone "deserves" a chance to sing in the play.

110

So today we spent an hour learning the worst song that's ever been written.

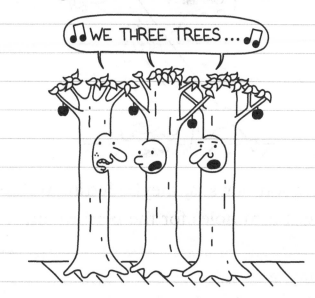

Thank God Rodrick won't be in the audience to see me humiliate myself. Mrs. Norton said the play is going to be a "semiformal occasion," and I know there's no way Rodrick is going to wear a tie for a middle school play.

But today wasn't all bad. Toward the end of practice, Archie Kelly tripped over Rodney James and chipped his tooth because he couldn't stick his arms out to break his fall.

So the good news is, they're letting us Trees carve out arm holes for the performance.

Tuesday
Tonight was the big school production of "The Wizard of Oz." The first sign that things were not going to go well happened before the play even started.

I was peeking through the curtain to check out how many people showed up to see the play, and guess who was standing right up front? My brother Rodrick, wearing a clip-on tie.

He must have found out I was singing, and he couldn't resist the chance to see me embarrass myself.

The play was supposed to start at 8:00, but it got delayed because Rodney James had stage fright.

You'd figure that someone whose job it was to sit on the stage and do nothing could just suck it up for one performance. But Rodney wouldn't budge, and eventually, his mom had to carry him off.

The play finally got started around 8:30. Nobody could remember their lines, just like I predicted, but Mrs. Norton kept things moving along with her piano.

The kid who played Toto brought a stool and a pile of comic books onto the stage, and that totally ruined the whole "dog" effect.

When it was time for the forest scene, me and the other Trees hopped into our positions. The curtains rose, and when they did, I heard Manny's voice.

Great. I have been able to keep that
nickname quiet for five years, and now
all of the sudden the whole town knew it.
I could feel about 300 pairs of eyeballs
pointed my way.

So I did some quick ad-libbing and I was
able to deflect the embarrassment over to
Archie Kelly.

But the major embarrassment was still
on the way. When I heard Mrs. Norton
playing the first few bars of "We Three
Trees," I felt my stomach jump.

I looked out at the audience, and I noticed
Rodrick was holding a video camera.

I knew that if I sang the song and Rodrick recorded it, he would keep the tape forever and use it to humiliate me for the rest of my life.

I didn't know what to do, so when the time came to start singing, I just kept my mouth shut.

WE THREE TREES FROM YONDER GLEN...

For a few seconds there, things went OK. I figured that if I didn't technically sing the song, then Rodrick wouldn't have anything to hold over my head. But after a few seconds, the other Trees noticed I wasn't singing.

I guess they must've thought I knew
something that they didn't, so they stopped
singing, too.

Now the three of us were just standing
there, not saying a word. Mrs. Norton
must have thought we forgot the words to
the song, because she came over to the side
of the stage and whispered the rest of the
lyrics to us.

The song is only about three minutes long, but to me it felt like an hour and a half. I was just praying the curtains would go down so we could hop off the stage.

That's when I noticed Patty Farrell standing in the wings. And if looks could kill, us Trees would be dead. She probably thought we were ruining her chances of making it to Broadway or something.

Seeing Patty standing there reminded me why I signed up to be a Tree in the first place.

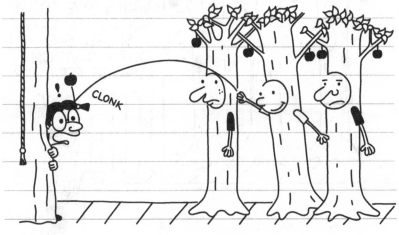

Pretty soon, the rest of the Trees started throwing apples, too. I think Toto even got in on the act.

Somebody knocked the glasses off of Patty's head, and one of the lenses broke. Mrs. Norton had to shut down the play after that, because Patty can't see two feet in front of her without her glasses.

After the play was over, my family went home together. Mom had brought a bouquet of flowers, and I guess they were supposed to be for me. But she ended up tossing them in the trash can on the way out the door.

I just hope that everyone who came to see the play was as entertained as I was.

Wednesday

Well, if one good thing came out of the play, it's that I don't have to worry about the "Bubby" nickname anymore.

I saw Archie Kelly getting hassled in the hallway after fifth period today, so it looks like I can finally start to breathe a little easier.

Sunday

With all this stuff going on at school, I haven't even had time to think about Christmas. And it's less than ten days away.

In fact, the only thing that tipped me off that Christmas was coming was when Rodrick put his wish list up on the refrigerator.

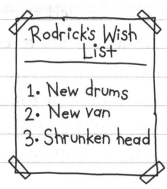

Rodrick's Wish List

1. New drums
2. New van
3. Shrunken head

I usually make a big wish list every year, but this Christmas, all I really want is this video game called Twisted Wizard.

Tonight Manny was going through the Christmas catalog, picking out all the stuff he wants with a big red marker. Manny was circling every single toy in the catalog. He was even circling really expensive things like a giant motorized car and stuff like that.

So I decided to step in and give him some good big-brotherly advice.

I told him that if he circled stuff that was too expensive, he was going to end up with a bunch of clothes for Christmas. I said he should just pick three or four medium-priced gifts so he would end up with a couple of things he actually wanted.

But of course Manny just went back to circling everything again. So I guess he'll just have to learn the hard way.

When I was seven, the only thing I really wanted for Christmas was a Barbie Dream House. And NOT because I like girls' toys, like Rodrick said.

I just thought it would be a really awesome fort for my toy soldiers.

When Mom and Dad saw my wish list that year, they got in a big fight over it. Dad said there was no way he was getting me a dollhouse, but Mom said it was healthy for me to "experiment" with whatever kind of toys I wanted to play with.

Believe it or not, Dad actually won that argument. Dad told me to start my wish list over and pick some toys that were more "appropriate" for boys.

But I have a secret weapon when it comes to Christmas. My Uncle Charlie always gets me whatever I want. I told him I wanted the Barbie Dream House, and he said he'd hook me up.

On Christmas, when Uncle Charlie gave me my gift, it was NOT what I asked for. He must've walked into the toy store and picked up the first thing he saw that had the word "Barbie" on it.

So if you ever see a picture of me where I'm holding a Beach Fun Barbie, now at least you know the whole story.

Dad wasn't real happy when he saw what Uncle Charlie got me. He told me to either throw it out or give it away to charity.

But I kept it anyway. And OK, I admit maybe I took it out and played with it once or twice.

That's how I ended up in the emergency room two weeks later with a pink Barbie shoe stuck up my nose. And believe me, Rodrick has never let me hear the end of THAT.

Thursday

Tonight me and Mom went out to get a gift for the Giving Tree at church. The Giving Tree is basically a Secret Santa kind of thing where you get a gift for someone who is needy.

Mom picked out a red wool sweater for our Giving Tree guy.

I tried to talk Mom into getting something a lot cooler, like a TV or a slushie machine or something like that.

Because imagine if all you got on Christmas was a wool sweater.

I'm sure our Giving Tree guy will throw his sweater in the trash, along with the ten cans of yams we sent his way during the Thanksgiving Food Drive.

## Christmas

When I woke up this morning and went downstairs, there were about a million gifts under the Christmas tree. But when I started digging around, there were hardly any gifts with my name on them.

But Manny made out like a bandit. He got EVERY single thing he circled in the catalog, no lie. So I'll bet he's glad he didn't listen to me.

I did find a couple things with my name on them, but they were mostly books and socks and stuff like that.

I opened my gifts in the corner behind the couch, because I don't like opening gifts near Dad. Whenever someone opens a gift, Dad swoops right in and cleans up after them.

I gave Manny a toy helicopter and I gave
Rodrick a book about rock bands. Rodrick
gave me a book, too, but of course he
didn't wrap it. The book he got me was
"Best of L'il Cutie." "L'il Cutie" is the
worst comic in the newspaper, and Rodrick
knows how much I hate it. I think this is
the fourth year in a row I've gotten a "L'il
Cutie" book from him.

I gave Mom and Dad their gifts. I get them
the same kind of thing every year, but
parents eat that stuff up.

The rest of the relatives started showing up around 11:00, and Uncle Charlie came at noon.

Uncle Charlie brought a big trash bag full of gifts, and he pulled my present out of the top of the bag.

The package was the exact right size and shape to be a Twisted Wizard game, so I knew Uncle Charlie came through for me. Mom got the camera ready and I tore open my gift.

But it was just an 8 x 10 picture of Uncle Charlie.

I guess I didn't do a good job of hiding my disappointment, and Mom got mad. All I can say is, I'm glad I'm still a kid, because if I had to act happy about the kinds of gifts grown-ups get, I don't think I could pull it off.

I went up to my room to take a break for a while. A couple minutes later, Dad knocked on my door. He told me he had my gift for me out in the garage, and the reason it was out there was because it was too big to wrap.

And when I walked down to the garage, there was a brand-new weight set.

That thing must have cost a fortune. I
didn't have the heart to tell Dad that I kind
of lost interest in the whole weight-lifting
thing when the wrestling unit ended last
week. So I just said "thanks" instead.

I think Dad was expecting me to drop
down and start doing some reps or
something, but I just excused myself and
went back inside.

At about 6:00, all the relatives cleared out.

I was sitting on the couch watching Manny
play with his toys, feeling pretty sorry for
myself. Then Mom came up to me and said
that she found a gift behind the piano with
my name on it, and it said, "From Santa."

The box was way too big for Twisted Wizard, but Mom pulled the same "big box" trick on me last year when she got me a memory card for my video game system.

So I ripped open the package and pulled out my present. Only this wasn't Twisted Wizard, either. It was a giant red wool sweater.

At first I thought Mom was playing some kind of practical joke on me, because this sweater was the same kind we bought for our Giving Tree guy.

But Mom seemed pretty confused, too. She said she DID buy me a video game, and that she had no idea what the sweater was doing in my box.

And then I figured it out. I told Mom there must have been some kind of mix-up, and I got the Giving Tree guy's gift, and he got mine.

Mom said she used the same kind of wrapping paper for both of our gifts, so she must've written the wrong names on the tags.

But then Mom said that this was really a good thing, because the Giving Tree guy was probably really happy he got such a great gift.

I had to explain that you need a game
system and a TV to play Twisted Wizard,
so the game was totally useless to him.

Even though my Christmas was not going
that great, I'm sure it was going a whole lot
worse for the Giving Tree guy.

I kind of decided to throw in the towel
for this Christmas, and I headed up to
Rowley's house.

I forgot to get a gift for Rowley, so I just slapped a bow on the "L'il Cutie" book Rodrick gave me.

And that seemed to do the trick.

Rowley's parents have a lot of money, so I can always count on them for a good gift.

But Rowley said that this year he picked out my gift himself. Then he brought me outside to show me what it was.

From the way Rowley was hyping his present, I thought he must have gotten me a big-screen TV or a motorcycle or something.

But once again, I let my hopes get too high.

Rowley got me a Big Wheel. I guess I would have thought this was a cool gift when I was in the third grade, but I have no idea what I'm supposed to do with one now.

Rowley was so enthusiastic about it that I tried my best to act like I was happy anyway.

We went back inside, and Rowley showed me his Christmas loot.

He sure got a lot more stuff than I did. He even got Twisted Wizard, so at least I can play it when I come up to his house. That is, until Rowley's dad finds out how violent it is.

And boy, you have never seen someone as happy as Rowley with his "L'il Cutie" book. His mom said it was the only thing on his list that he didn't get.

Well, I'm glad SOMEONE got what they wanted today.

IT'S A CHRISTMAS MIRACLE!

New Year's Eve

In case you're wondering what I'm doing in my room at 9:00 p.m. on New Year's Eve, let me fill you in.

Earlier today, me and Manny were horsing around in the basement. I found a tiny black ball of thread on the carpet, and I told Manny it was a spider.

Then I held it over him pretending like I was going to make him eat it.

Right when I was about to let Manny go, he slapped my hand and made me drop the thread. And guess what? That fool swallowed it.

Well, Manny completely lost his mind. He ran upstairs to where Mom was, and I knew I was in big trouble.

Manny told Mom I made him eat a spider. I told her there was no spider, and that it was just a tiny ball of thread.

Mom brought Manny over to the kitchen table. Then she put a seed, a raisin, and a grape on a plate and told Manny to point to the thing that was the closest in size to the piece of thread he swallowed.

Manny took a while to look over the things on the plate.

Then he walked over to the refrigerator and pulled out an orange.

So that's why I got sent to bed at 7:00 and I'm not downstairs watching the New Year's Eve special on TV.

And that's also why my only New Year's resolution is to never play with Manny again.

<u>Wednesday</u>

I found a way to have some fun with the Big Wheel Rowley got me for Christmas. I came up with this game where one guy rides down the hill and the other guy tries to knock him off with a football.

Rowley was the first one down the hill, and I was the thrower.

It's a lot harder to hit a moving target than I thought. Plus, I didn't get a lot of practice. It took Rowley like ten minutes to walk the Big Wheel back up the hill after every trip down.

142

Rowley kept asking to switch places and have me be the one who rides the Big Wheel, but I'm no fool. That thing was hitting thirty-five miles an hour, and it didn't have any brakes.

Anyway, I never did knock Rowley off the Big Wheel today. But I guess I have something to work at over the rest of Christmas vacation.

<u>Thursday</u>
I was heading up to Rowley's today to play our Big Wheel game again, but Mom said I had to finish my Christmas thank-yous before I went out anywhere.

I thought I could just crank out my thank-you cards in a half hour, but when it came to actually writing them, my mind went blank.

Let me tell you, it's not easy writing thank-you notes for stuff you didn't want in the first place.

I started with the nonclothes items, because I thought they'd be easiest. But after two or three cards, I realized I was practically writing the same thing every time.

So I wrote up a general form on the computer with blanks for the things that needed to change. Writing the cards from there was a breeze.

TYPE
TYPE

Dear Aunt Lydia,

Thank you so much for the awesome encyclopedia !
How did you know I wanted that for Christmas?

I love the way the encyclopedia looks on my shelf !

All my friends will be so jealous that I have my very own
encyclopedia .

Thank you for making this the best Christmas ever!

Sincerely, Greg

My system worked out pretty well for the first couple of gifts, but after that, not so much.

Dear Aunt Loretta,

Thank you so much for the awesome pants !
How did you know I wanted that for Christmas?

I love the way the pants looks on my legs !

All my friends will be so jealous that I have my very own
pants .

Thank you for making this the best Christmas ever!

Sincerely, Greg

<u>Friday</u>

I finally knocked Rowley off the Big Wheel today, but it didn't happen the way I expected. I was trying to hit him in the shoulder, but I missed, and the football went under the front tire.

Rowley tried to break his fall by sticking out his arms, but he landed pretty hard on his left hand. I figured he'd just shake it off and get right back on the bike, but he didn't.

I tried to cheer him up, but all the jokes that usually crack him up weren't working.

So I knew he must be hurt pretty bad.

## Monday

Christmas vacation is over, and now we're
back at school. And you remember Rowley's
Big Wheel accident? Well, he broke his
hand, and now he has to wear a cast. And
today, everyone was crowding around him
like he was a hero or something.

I tried to cash in on some of Rowley's new popularity, but it totally backfired.

At lunch a bunch of girls invited Rowley over to their table so they could FEED him.

What really ticks me off about that is that Rowley is right-handed, and it's his LEFT hand that's broken. So he can feed himself just fine.

<u>Tuesday</u>

I realized Rowley's injury thing is a pretty good racket, so I decided it was time for me to have an injury of my own.

I took some gauze from home, and I wrapped up my hand to make it look like it was hurt.

I couldn't figure out why the girls weren't swarming me like they swarmed Rowley, but then I realized what the problem was.

See, the cast is a great gimmick because everyone wants to sign their name on it. But it's not exactly easy to sign gauze with a pen.

So I came up with a solution that I thought was just as good.

That idea was a total bust, too. My bandage did end up attracting attention from a couple of people, but believe me, they were not the type of people I was going for.

<u>Monday</u>

Last week we started the third quarter at school, so now I have a whole bunch of new classes. One of the classes I signed up for is something called Independent Study.

I WANTED to sign up for Home Economics 2, because I was pretty good at Home Ec 1.

But being good at sewing does not exactly buy you popularity points at school.

Anyway, this Independent Study thing is an experiment they're trying out at our school for the first time.

The idea is that the class gets assigned a project, and then you have to work on it together with no teacher in the room for the whole quarter.

The catch is that when you're done, everyone in your group gets the same grade. I found out that Ricky Fisher is in my class, which could be a big problem.

Ricky's big claim to fame is that he'll pick the gum off the bottom of a desk and chew it if you pay him fifty cents. So I don't really have high hopes for our final grade.

Tuesday
Today we got our Independent Study assignment, and guess what it is? We have to build a robot.

At first everybody kind of freaked out, because we thought we were going to have to build the robot from scratch.

But Mr. Darnell told us we don't have to build an actual robot. We just need to come up with ideas for what our robot might look like and what kinds of things it would be able to do.

Then he left the room, and we were on our own. We started brainstorming right away. I wrote down a bunch of ideas on the blackboard.

the robot would
do my homework
do the dishes
make my break-
fast
brush my teeth

Everybody was pretty impressed with my ideas, but it was easy to come up with them. All I did was write down all the things I hate doing myself.

But a couple of the girls got up to the front of the room, and they had some ideas of their own. They erased my list and drew up their own plan.

They wanted to invent a robot that would give you dating advice and have ten types of lip gloss on its fingertips.

All us guys thought this was the stupidest idea we ever heard. So we ended up splitting into two groups, girls and boys. The boys went to the other side of the room while the girls stood around talking.

Now that we had all the serious workers in one place, we got to work. Someone had the idea that you can say your name to the robot and it can say it back to you.

But then someone else pointed out that you shouldn't be able to use bad words for your name, because the robot shouldn't be able to curse. So we decided we should come up with a list of all the bad words the robot shouldn't be able to say.

We came up with all the regular bad words, but then Ricky Fisher came up with twenty more the rest of us had never even heard before.

So Ricky ended up being one of the most valuable contributors on this project.

Right before the bell rang, Mr. Darnell came back in the room to check on our progress. He picked up the piece of paper we were writing on and read it over.

To make a long story short, Independent Study is canceled for the rest of the year.

Well, at least it is for us boys. So if the robots in the future are going around with cherry lip gloss for fingers, at least now you know how it all got started.

Thursday
In school today they had a general assembly and showed the movie "It's Great to Be Me," which they show us every year.

The movie is all about how you should be happy with who you are and not change anything about yourself.

To be honest with you, I think that's a really dumb message to be telling kids, especially the ones at my school.

Later on, they made an announcement that there are some openings on the Safety Patrols, and that got me thinking.

If someone picks on a Safety Patrol, it can get them suspended. The way I figure it, I can use any extra protection I can get.

Plus, I realized that maybe being in a position of authority could be good for me.

I went down to Mr. Winsky's office and signed myself up, and I got Rowley to sign up, too. I thought Mr. Winsky would make us do a bunch of chin-ups or jumping jacks or something to prove we were up for the job, but he just handed us our belts and badges on the spot.

Mr. Winsky said the openings were for a special assignment. Our school is right next to the elementary school, and they've got a half-day kindergarten there.

He wants us to walk the morning session kids home in the middle of the day. I realized that meant we would miss twenty minutes of Pre-Algebra. Rowley must have figured that out, too, because he started to speak up. But I gave him a wicked pinch underneath the desk before he could finish his sentence.

BUT WE WOULD MISS YAHOOEY!

I couldn't believe my luck. I was getting instant bully protection and a free pass from half of Pre-Algebra, and I didn't even have to lift a finger.

Today was our first day as Safety Patrols. Me and Rowley don't technically have stations like all the other Patrols, so that means we don't have to stand out in the freezing cold for an hour before school.

But that didn't stop us from coming to the cafeteria for the free hot chocolate they hand out to the other Patrols before homeroom.

Another great perk is that you get to show up ten minutes late for first period.

HEL-LO!

I'm telling you, I've got it made with this Safety Patrol thing.

At 12:15, me and Rowley left school and walked the kindergartners home. The whole trip ate up forty-five minutes, and there were only twenty minutes of Pre-Algebra left when we got back.

Walking the kids home was no sweat. But one of the kindergartners started to smell a little funny, and I think maybe he had an accident in his pants.

He tried to let me know about it, but I just stared straight ahead and kept walking. I'll take these kids home, but believe me, I didn't sign up for any diaper duty.

<u>Wednesday</u>

Today it snowed for the first time this winter, and school was canceled. We were supposed to have a test in Pre-Algebra, and I've kind of slacked off ever since I became a Safety Patrol. So I was psyched.

I called Rowley and told him to come over. Me and him have been talking about building the world's biggest snowman for the past couple of years now.

And when I say the world's biggest snowman, I'm not kidding. Our goal is to get into the "Guinness Book of World Records."

162

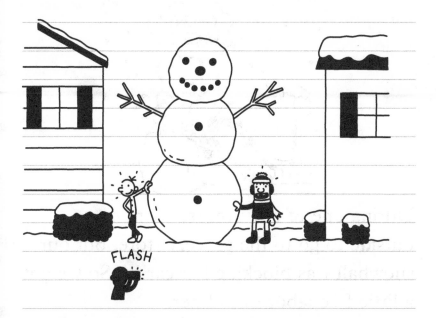

FLASH

But every time we've gotten serious about going for the record, all the snow has melted, and we've missed our window of opportunity. So this year, I wanted to get started right away.

When Rowley came over, we started rolling the first snowball to make the base. I figured the base was going to have to be at least eight feet tall on its own if we wanted to have a shot at breaking the record. But the snowball got real heavy, and we had to take a bunch of breaks in between rolls so we could catch our breath.

During one of our breaks, Mom came outside to go to the grocery store, but our snowball was blocking her car in. So we got a little free labor out of her.

After our break, me and Rowley pushed that snowball until we couldn't push it any farther. But when we looked behind us, we saw the mess we had made.

The snowball had gotten so heavy that it tore up all the sod Dad had just laid down this fall.

I was hoping it would snow a few more inches and cover up our tracks, but just like that, it stopped snowing.

Our plan to build the world's biggest snowman was starting to fall apart. So I came up with a better idea for our snowball.

Every time it snows, the kids from Whirley Street use our hill for sledding, even though this isn't their neighborhood.

So tomorrow morning, when the Whirley Street kids come marching up our hill, me and Rowley are going to teach those guys a lesson.

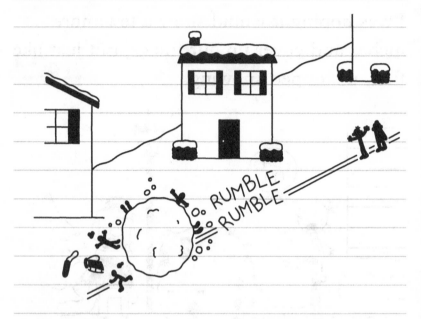

Thursday

When I woke up this morning, the snow was already starting to melt. So I told Rowley to hurry up and get down to my house.

While I was waiting for Rowley to show up, I watched Manny trying to build a snowman out of the piddly crumbs of snow that were left over from our snowball.

166

It was actually kind of pathetic.

I really couldn't help doing what I did next. Unfortunately for me, right at that moment, Dad was at the front window.

Dad was ALREADY mad at me for tearing up the sod, so I knew I was in for it. I heard the garage door open and I saw Dad coming outside. He marched right out carrying a snow shovel, and I thought I was going to have to make a run for it.

But Dad was heading for my snowball, not me. And in less than a minute, he reduced all our hard work to nothing.

Rowley came by a few minutes later. I thought he might actually get a kick out of what happened.

But I guess he had his heart set on rolling that snowball down the hill, and he was really mad. But get this: Rowley was mad at ME for what DAD did.

I told Rowley he was being a big baby, and we got in a shoving match. Right when it looked like we were going to get in an all-out fight, we got ambushed from the street.

It was a hit-and-run by the Whirley Street kids.

And if Mrs. Levine, my English teacher, was there, I'm sure she would have said the whole situation was "ironic."

Wednesday
Today at school they announced there's an opening for the cartoonist job in the school paper. There's only one comic slot, and up until now this kid named Bryan Little has been hogging it all to himself.

Bryan has this comic called "Wacky Dawg," and when it started off, it was actually pretty funny.

But lately, Bryan's been using his strip to handle his personal business. I guess that's why they gave him the axe.

Wacky Dawg                                  Bryan Little

As soon as I heard the news, I knew I had to try out. "Wacky Dawg" made Bryan Little a celebrity at our school, and I wanted to get in on some of that kind of fame.

I had a taste of what it's like to be famous at my school when I won honorable mention in this antismoking contest they had.

All I did was trace a picture from one of Rodrick's heavy metal magazines, but luckily, no one ever found out.

The kid who won first place is named Chris Carney. And what kind of ticks me off is that Chris smokes at least a pack of cigarettes a day.

<u>Thursday</u>

Me and Rowley decided to team up and do a cartoon together. So after school today he came over to my house, and we got to work.

We banged out a bunch of characters real quick, but that turned out to be the easy part. When we tried to think up some jokes, we kind of hit a wall.

I finally came up with a good solution.

I made up a cartoon where the punch line of every strip is "Zoo-Wee Mama!"

That way we wouldn't get bogged down with having to write actual jokes, and we could concentrate on the pictures.

For the first couple of strips, I did the writing and drew the characters, and Rowley drew the boxes around the pictures.

Rowley started complaining that he didn't have enough to do, so I let him write a few of the strips.

But to be honest with you, there was a pretty obvious drop in quality once Rowley started doing the writing.

Eventually I got kind of sick of the "Zoo-Wee Mama" idea and I pretty much let Rowley take over the whole operation.

And believe it or not, Rowley's drawing skills are worse than his writing skills.

I told Rowley maybe we should come up with some new ideas, but he just wanted to keep writing "Zoo-Wee Mamas." Then he packed up his comics and went home, which was fine by me. I don't really want to be partnered up with a kid who doesn't draw noses, anyway.

Friday

After Rowley left yesterday, I really got to work on some comics. I came up with this character called Creighton the Cretin, and I got on a roll.

CREIGHTON THE CRETIN        by Greg Heffley

HI, MY NAME IS CREIGHTON.

NO IT ISN'T. YOUR NAME IS "STEWART PID."

OOPS. HI, I'M STEW PID.

HAR HAR HAR HAR!

?

I must've banged out twenty strips, and I didn't even break a sweat.

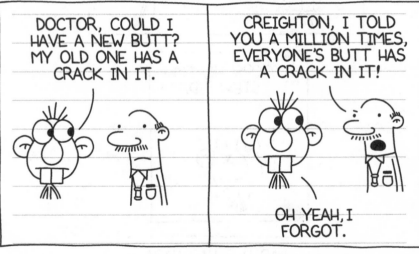

The great thing about these "Creighton the Cretin" comics is that with all the idiots running around my school, I will NEVER run out of new material.

178

When I got to school today, I took my comics to Mr. Ira's office. He's the teacher who runs the school newspaper.

But when I went to turn my strips in, I saw that there was a pile of comics from other kids who were trying out for the job.

Most of them were pretty bad, so I wasn't too worried about the competition.

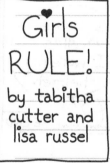

One of the comics was called "Dumb Teachers," and it was written by this kid named Bill Tritt.

Bill is always in detention, so I guess he has a bone to pick with just about every teacher in the school, including Mr. Ira.

So I'm not too worried about the chances of Bill's comic getting in, either.

There were actually one or two decent comics in the bin. But I slipped them under a pile of paperwork on Mr. Ira's desk.

Hopefully, those ones won't turn up until I'm in high school.

<u>Thursday</u>

Today, during morning announcements, I got the news I was hoping for.

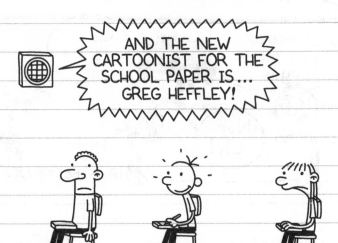

The paper came out today at lunch time, and everyone was reading it.

I really wanted to pick up a copy to see my name in print, but I decided to just play it cool for a while instead.

I sat at the end of the lunch table so there would be plenty of room for me to start signing autographs for my new fans. But nobody was coming over to tell me how great my comic was, and I started to get the feeling something was wrong.

I grabbed a paper and went into the bathroom to check it out. And when I saw my comic, I practically had a heart attack.

Mr. Ira told me he had made some "minor edits" to my comic. I thought he just meant he fixed spelling mistakes and stuff like that, but he totally butchered it.

The comic he ruined was one of my favorite ones, too. In the original, Creighton the Cretin is taking a math test, and he accidentally eats it. And then the teacher yells at him for being such a moron.

By the time Mr. Ira was done with it, you practically couldn't recognize it as the same strip.

Creighton the Curious Student                    by Gregory Heffley

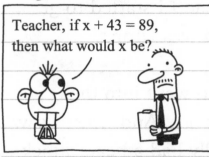

So I'm pretty sure I won't be signing autographs anytime soon.

<u>Wednesday</u>

Me and Rowley were enjoying our hot chocolate in the cafeteria with the rest of the Patrols today, and there was an announcement on the loudspeaker.

Rowley went down to Mr. Winsky's office, and when Rowley came back fifteen minutes later, he looked pretty shaken up.

Apparently Mr. Winsky got a call from a parent who said they witnessed Rowley "terrorizing" the kindergartners when he was supposed to be walking them home from school. And Mr. Winsky was really mad about it.

Rowley said Mr. Winsky yelled at him for about ten minutes and said his actions "disrespected the badge."

You know, I think I might just know what this is all about. Last week, Rowley had to take a quiz during fourth period, so I walked the kindergartners home on my own.

It had rained that morning, and there were a lot of worms on the sidewalk. So I decided to have some fun with the kids.

But some neighborhood lady saw what I was doing, and she yelled at me from her front porch.

It was Mrs. Irvine, who is friends with Rowley's mom. She must have thought I was Rowley, because I was borrowing his coat. And I wasn't about to correct her, either.

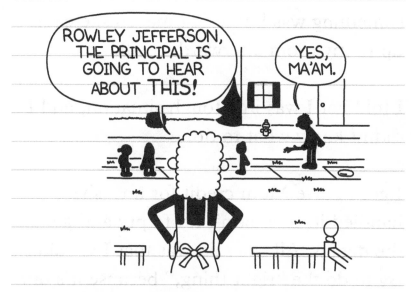

I forgot about the whole incident until today.

Anyway, Mr. Winsky told Rowley he's going to have to apologize to the kindergartners tomorrow morning, and that he's suspended from Patrols for a week.

I knew I should probably just tell Mr. Winsky it was me who chased the kids with the worms. But I wasn't ready to set the record straight just yet. I knew if I confessed, I'd lose my hot chocolate privileges. And that right there was enough to make me keep quiet for the time being.

At dinner tonight, Mom could tell something was bothering me, so she came up to my room afterward to talk.

I told her I was in a tough situation, and I didn't know what to do.

I got to give Mom credit for how she handled it. She didn't try to pry and get all the details. All she said was that I should try to do the "right thing," because it's our choices that make us who we are.

I figure that's pretty decent advice. But I'm still not 100% sure what I'm going to do tomorrow.

Thursday

Well, I was up all night tossing and turning over this Rowley situation, but I finally made up my mind. I decided the right thing to do was to just let Rowley take one for the team this time around.

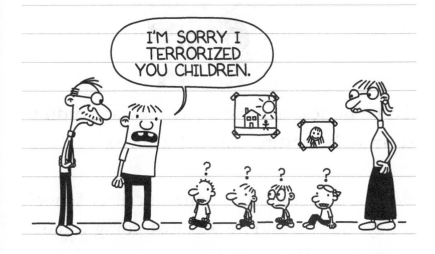

On the way home from school, I came clean with Rowley and told him the whole truth about what happened, and how it was me who chased the kids with the worms.

Then I told him there were lessons we could both learn from this. I told him I learned to be more careful about what I do in front of Mrs. Irvine's house, and that he learned a valuable lesson, too, which is this: Be careful about who you lend your coat to.

To be honest with you, my message didn't seem to be getting through to Rowley.

We were supposed to hang out after school today, but he said he was just going to go home and take a nap.

I couldn't really blame him. Because if I didn't have my hot chocolate this morning, I wouldn't have had much energy, either.

When I got home, Mom was waiting for me at the front door.

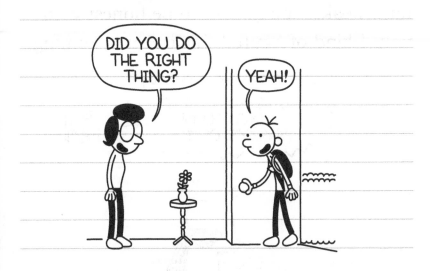

Mom took me out to get some ice cream as a special treat. And what this whole episode has taught me is that every once in a while, it's not such a bad idea to listen to your mother.

<u>Tuesday</u>

There was another announcement on the loudspeaker today, and to be honest with you, I kind of figured this one was coming.

I knew it was just a matter of time before I got busted for what happened last week.

When I got to Mr. Winsky's office, he was really mad. Mr. Winsky told me that an "anonymous source" had informed him that I was the real culprit in the worm-chasing incident.

Then he told me I was relieved of my Safety Patrol duties "effective immediately."

Well, it doesn't take a detective to figure out that the anonymous source was Rowley.

I can't believe Rowley went and backstabbed me like that. While I was sitting there getting chewed out by Mr. Winsky, I was thinking, I need to remember to give my friend a lecture about loyalty.

Later on today, Rowley got reinstated as a Patrol. And get this: He actually got a PROMOTION. Mr. Winsky said Rowley had "exhibited dignity under false suspicion."

I thought about really letting Rowley have it for ratting me out like that, but then I realized something.

In June, all the officers in the Safety Patrols go on a trip to Six Flags, and they get to take along one friend. I need to make sure Rowley knows I'm his guy.

LET ME GET THIS FOR YOU, "CAPTAIN"!

Tuesday
Like I said before, the worst part of getting kicked off Safety Patrols is losing your hot chocolate privileges.

Every morning, I go to the back door of the cafeteria so Rowley can hook me up.

But either my friend has gone deaf or he's too busy kissing the other officers' butts to notice me at the window.

In fact, now that I think of it, Rowley has been TOTALLY giving me the cold shoulder lately. And that's really lame, because if I recall correctly, HE's the one that sold ME out.

Even though Rowley has been a total jerk lately, I tried to break the ice with him today, anyway. But even THAT didn't seem to work.

<u>Friday</u>

Ever since the worm incident, Rowley has been hanging out with Collin Lee every day after school. What really stinks is that Collin is supposed to be MY backup friend.

Those guys are acting totally ridiculous. Today, Rowley and Collin were wearing these matching T-shirts, and it made me just about want to vomit.

After dinner tonight, I saw Rowley and Collin walking up the hill together, chumming it up.

Collin had his overnight bag, so I knew they were going to do a sleepover at Rowley's.

And I thought, Well, two can play at THAT game. The best way to get back at Rowley was to get a new best friend of my own. But unfortunately, the only person who came to mind right at that moment was Fregley.

I went up to Fregley's with my overnight bag so Rowley could see I had other friend options, too.

When I got there, Fregley was in his front yard stabbing a kite with a stick. That's when I started to think maybe this wasn't the best idea after all.

But Rowley was in his front yard, and he was watching me. So I knew there was no turning back.

I invited myself into Fregley's house. His mom said she was excited to see Fregley with a "playmate," which was a term I was not too enthusiastic about.

Me and Fregley went upstairs to his room. Fregley tried to get me to play Twister with him, so I made sure I stayed ten feet away from him at all times.

I decided that I should just pull the plug on this stupid idea and go home. But every time I looked out the window, Rowley and Collin were still in Rowley's front yard.

I didn't want to leave until those guys went back inside. But things started to get out of hand with Fregley pretty quickly. When I was looking out the window, Fregley broke into my backpack and ate the whole bag of jelly beans I had in there.

Fregley's one of these kids who's not supposed to eat any sugar, so two minutes later, he was bouncing off the walls.

Fregley started acting like a total maniac, and he chased me all around his upstairs.

I kept thinking he was going to come down off of his sugar high, but he didn't. Eventually, I locked myself in his bathroom to wait him out.

Around 11:30, it got quiet out in the hallway. That's when Fregley slipped a piece of paper under the door.

I picked it up and read it.

That's the last thing I remember before I blacked out.

I came to my senses a few hours later. After I woke up, I cracked the door open, and I heard snoring coming from Fregley's room. So I decided to make a run for it.

Mom and Dad were not happy with me for getting them out of bed at 2:00 in the morning. But by that point, I could really care less.

Well, me and Rowley have officially been ex-friends for about a month now, and to be honest with you, I'm better off without him.

I'm glad I can just do whatever I want without having to worry about carrying all that dead weight around.

Lately I've been hanging out in Rodrick's room after school and going through his stuff. The other day, I found one of his middle school yearbooks.

Rodrick wrote on everybody's picture in his yearbook, so you can tell how he felt about all the kids in his grade.

202

Every once in a while, I see Rodrick's old classmates around town. And I have to remember to thank Rodrick for making church a lot more interesting.

But the page in Rodrick's yearbook that's really interesting is the Class Favorites page.

That's where they put pictures of the kids who get voted Most Popular and Most Talented and all that.

Rodrick wrote on his Class Favorites page, too.

## MOST LIKELY TO SUCCEED

Bill Watson        Kathy Nguyen

You know, this Class Favorites thing has really got my gears turning.

If you can get yourself voted onto the Class Favorites page, you're practically an immortal. Even if you don't live up to what you got picked for, it doesn't really matter, because it's on permanent record.

People still treat Bill Watson like he's something special, even though he ended up dropping out of high school.

We still run into him at the Food Barn every once in a while.

So here's what I'm thinking: This school year has been kind of a bust, but if I can get voted as a Class Favorite, I'll go out on a high note.

I've been trying to think of a category I have a shot at. Most Popular and Most Athletic are definitely out, so I'm going to have to find something that's a little bit more in reach.

At first I thought maybe I should wear really nice clothes for the rest of the year so I can get Best Dressed.

But that would mean I would have to get my picture taken with Jenna Stewart, and she dresses like a Pilgrim.

<u>Wednesday</u>

Last night I was lying in bed, and it hit me: I should go for Class Clown.

It's not like I'm known for being real funny at school or anything, but if I can pull off one big prank right before voting, that could do it.

<u>Thursday</u>

Today I was trying to figure out how I was going to sneak a thumbtack onto Mr. Worth's chair in History when he said something that made me rethink my plan.

Mr. Worth told us he has a dentist's appointment tomorrow, so we're going to have a substitute. Subs are like comic gold. You can say just about anything you want, and you can't get in trouble.

I walked into my History class today, ready to execute my plan. But when I got to the door, guess who the substitute teacher was?

Of all the people in the world to be our sub today, it was Mom. I thought Mom's days of getting involved at my school were over.

She used to be one of those parents who came in to help out in the classroom. But that all changed after Mom volunteered to be a chaperone for our field trip to the zoo when I was in third grade.

Mom had prepared all sorts of material to help us kids appreciate the different exhibits, but all anyone wanted to do was watch the animals go to the bathroom.

Anyway, Mom totally foiled my plan to win Class Clown. I'm just lucky there's not a category called Biggest Mama's Boy, because after today, I'd win that one in a landslide.

## Wednesday

The school paper came out again today.
I quit my job as school cartoonist after
"Creighton the Curious Student" came
out, and I didn't really care who they
picked to replace me.

But everyone was laughing at the comics
page at lunch, so I picked up a copy to see
what was so funny. And when I opened it
up, I couldn't believe my eyes.

It was "Zoo-Wee Mama." And of course
Mr. Ira didn't change a single WORD of
Rowley's strip.

Zoo-Wee Mama            by Rowley Jefferson

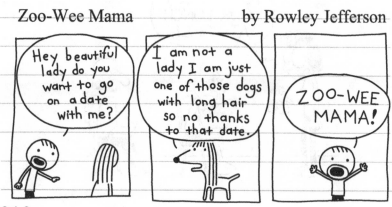

So now Rowley's getting all the fame that was supposed to be mine.

Even the teachers are kissing Rowley's butt. I almost lost my lunch when Mr. Worth dropped his chalk in History class —

<u>Monday</u>

This "Zoo-Wee Mama" thing has really got me worked up. Rowley is getting all the credit for a comic that we came up with together. I figured the least he could do was put my name on the strip as the co-creator.

So I went up to Rowley after school and told him that's what he was gonna have to do. But Rowley said "Zoo-Wee Mama" was all HIS idea and that I didn't have anything to do with it.

I guess we must've been talking pretty loud, because the next thing you knew, we attracted a crowd.

FIGHT! FIGHT! FIGHT!

FIGHT! FIGHT! FIGHT!

The kids at my school are ALWAYS itching to see a fight. Me and Rowley tried to walk away, but those guys weren't going to let us go until they saw us throw some punches.

I've never been in a real fight before, so I didn't know how I was supposed to stand or hold my fists or anything. And you could tell Rowley didn't know what he was doing either, because he just started prancing around like a leprechaun.

I was pretty sure I could take Rowley in a fight, but the thing that made me nervous was the fact that Rowley takes karate. I don't know what kind of hocus-pocus they teach in Rowley's karate classes, but the last thing I needed was for him to lay me out right there on the blacktop.

Before me or Rowley made a move, there was a screeching sound in the school parking lot. A bunch of teenagers had stopped their pickup truck, and they started piling out.

I was just happy that everyone's attention was on the teenagers instead of me and Rowley. But all the other kids took off when the teenagers started heading our way.

And then I realized that these teenagers looked awfully familiar.

That's when it hit me. These were the same guys who chased me and Rowley around on Halloween night, and they had finally caught up with us.

214

But before we could make a run for it, we had our arms pinned behind our backs.

Those guys wanted to teach us a lesson for taunting them on Halloween night, and they started arguing over what they should do with us.

But to be honest with you, I was more concerned about something else. The Cheese was only a few feet from where we were standing on the blacktop, and it was looking nastier than ever.

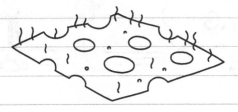

The big teenager must have caught my eye, because the next thing I knew, he was looking at the Cheese, too. And I guess that gave him the idea he was looking for.

Rowley got singled out first. The big kid grabbed Rowley and dragged him over to the Cheese.

Now, I don't want to say exactly what happened next. Because if Rowley ever tries to run for President and someone finds out what these guys made him do, he won't have a chance.

So I'll put it to you this way: They made Rowley _ _ _ the Cheese.

I knew they were gonna make me do it, too. I started to panic, because I knew I wasn't going to be able to fight my way out of this situation.

So I did some fast talking instead.

And believe it or not, it actually worked.

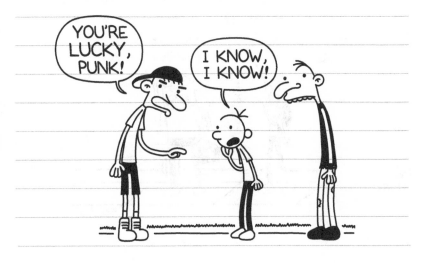

I guess the teenagers were satisfied they had made their point, because after they made Rowley finish off the rest of the Cheese, they let us go. They got back in their truck and took off down the road.

Me and Rowley walked home together. But neither one of us really said anything on the way back.

I thought about mentioning to Rowley that maybe he could have pulled out a couple of his karate moves back there, but something told me to hold off on that thought for right now.

At school today, the teachers let us outside after lunch.

It took about five seconds for someone to realize the Cheese was missing from its spot on the blacktop.

Everybody crowded 'nd to look at where the Cheese us 'o be. Nobody could believe it was actually gone.

People started coming up with these crazy theories about what happened to it. Somebody said that maybe the Cheese grew legs and walked away.

It took all my self-control to keep my mouth shut. And if Rowley wasn't standing right there, I honestly don't know if I could have kept quiet.

A couple of the guys who were arguing over what happened to the Cheese were the same ones who were egging me and Rowley on yesterday aftern    So I knew it wasn't going to be long b     someone put two and two together a   ured out that we must have had som     g to do with it.

Rowley was starting to panic, and I don't blame him, either. If the truth ever came out about how the Cheese disappeared, Rowley would be finished. He'd have to move out of the state, and maybe even the country.

220

That's when I decided to speak up.

I told everyone that I knew what happened to the Cheese. I said I was sick of it being on the blacktop, and I just decided to get rid of it once and for all.

For a second there, everyone just froze. I thought people were going to start thanking me for what I did, but boy, was I wrong.

I really wish I had worded my story a little differently. Because if I threw away the Cheese, guess what that meant? It meant that I have the Cheese Touch.

Friday

Well, if Rowley appreciated what I did for him last week, he hasn't said it. But we've started hanging out after school again, so I guess that means me and him are back to normal.

DIAPER RASH AHEAD!

BWAAHAHAHA!

I can honestly say that so far, having the Cheese Touch hasn't been all that bad.

It got me out of doing the Square Dance unit in Phys Ed, because no one would partner up with me. And I've had the whole lunch table to myself every day.

Today was the last day of school, and they handed out yearbooks after eighth period.

I flipped to the Class Favorites page, and here's the picture that was waiting for me.

## CLASS CLOWN

Rowley Jefferson

All I can say is, if anyone wants a free yearbook, they can dig one out of the trash can in the back of the cafeteria.

You know, Rowley can have Class Clown for all I care. But if he ever gets too big for his britches, I'll just remind him that he was the guy who ate the _ _ _ _ _ _.

# ACKNOWLEDGMENTS

There are many people who helped bring this book to life, but four individuals deserve special thanks:

Abrams editor Charlie Kochman, whose advocacy for *Diary of a Wimpy Kid* has been beyond what I could have hoped for. Any writer would be lucky to have Charlie as an editor.

Jess Brallier, who understands the power and potential of online publishing, and helped Greg Heffley reach the masses for the first time. Thanks especially for your friendship and mentorship.

Patrick, who was instrumental in helping me improve this book, and who wasn't afraid to tell me when a joke stunk.

My wife, Julie, without whose incredible support this book would not have become a reality.

# ABOUT THE AUTHOR

**Jeff Kinney** is a #1 *New York Times* bestselling author and a six-time Nickelodeon Kids' Choice Award winner for Favorite Book. Jeff has been named one of *Time* magazine's 100 Most Influential People in the World. He is also the creator of Poptropica, which was named one of *Time* magazine's 50 Best Websites. He spent his childhood in the Washington, D.C., area and moved to New England in 1995. Jeff lives with his wife and two sons in Massachusetts, where they own a bookstore, An Unlikely Story.